W9-AVS-738

PAUSE FOR THOUGHT

PAUSE FOR THOUGHT

✤ ✤ ✤

Foreword by
TERRY WOGAN

Edited by
LAVINIA BYRNE

Hodder & Stoughton

First published in Great Britain in 2002,
by arrangement with the BBC.

Pause for Thought is based on the BBC Radio 2 programme.

BBC Radio 2 word mark and logo are trademarks of the
British Broadcasting Corporation and are used under licence.
BBC logo copyright © 1996.

10 9 8 7 6 5 4 3 2

British Library Cataloguing in Publication Data
A record for this book is available from the British Library

ISBN 0 340 86107 X

Printed and bound in Great Britain by Clays Ltd, St Ives, plc

Hodder & Stoughton
A Division of Hodder Headline Ltd
338 Euston Road
London NW1 3BH
www.madaboutbooks.com

FOREWORD

The other day, a kindly listener reminded me that it was thirty years ago that I first presented the breakfast show on Radio 2. The gentle listener added that it seemed more like sixty, but you get the kind of listener you deserve. Thirty years. I would have got less for mass murder. I'll admit it now, but only to you, because you've got a kind face: I've loved every foolish, eccentric, laughter-filled minute of it. Sitting there in front of a microphone may seem a lonely, even loony, existence, but I feel I've made millions of friends. And if I lift the spirits of even one person on whom the day is weighing heavily, then I've done my job. That's why 'Pause for Thought' is such an integral part of *Wake Up to Wogan*. For a precious few minutes, it halts my incessant gabble, and gives people time to think. There's no preaching on 'Pause for Thought', no God-Bothering, no storming of heaven. It's an offering by Hindu and Christian, Catholic and Muslim, Buddhist and Sikh, Jew and Bahai. It's a prayer.

I've grown to know, respect and like all the contributors that feature in this splendid collection. I've known Brian D'Arcy since he was a boy – and he still looks like one; Ruth Scott in full clown's make-up; Rob Gillion fresh from driving a bus around London, advertising God; Rose Hudson-Wilkin sleeping out on her church roof; Murray Grant driving us all mad with jealousy with his tales of Neapolitan life and sunshine; Roger Royle frightening the horses with that snorting laugh; Pauline and Indarjit, Roy and John; Dharmachari Nagaraja, the gentle Scots Buddhist; Fidelma, the Bahai who has never seen their magnificent temple in Delhi; Oliver McTernan, from Notting Hill to Harvard. It seems to me as if I've seen Charles King's daughters grow up, yet I've never met them. David Cooper, Chaplain at Eton and former Marine Commando, is not in this book, because he delivers his 'thought' right off the top of his head. Rabbi Y.Y. Rubinstein had all his thoughts eaten by a computer bug. We miss them both.

Read this book. Dip in, when the mood takes you. It won't tell you what to think, it probably won't change your life. But it will give you pause. These are the thoughts of good people. The best kind of prayers.

Terry Wogan

Words can sometimes be hard to find. But sometimes the simplest and briefest of prayers can be profound: God of love, turn our hearts to your ways and give us peace, Amen.

Archbishop George Carey

✣ ✣ ✣

Sometimes silence is better than words. In the silence we can have space to hold what has happened in our hearts and to cry.

May all beings be well; may all beings be happy; may all beings be free from suffering.

Dharmachari Nagaraja

✣ ✣ ✣

When I was first learning the ropes as a priest, I was taken to Basingstoke Hospital by the vicar of my training parish, to do some visiting. He said, 'Go and see Mrs Lawrence. She is very elderly, in a coma, and has not responded to anyone for weeks.' I found her in the last bed at the end of the ward. She looked so frail and so alone. What was I to do? Well, my training manual suggested I make contact with the patient. So I said, 'Hello!' No response. I then took her hand – but still no response. I felt so awkward. I knew I ought to pray with her but I didn't have a prayer about being in a coma. My prayer was 'O Lord, help me!' and then I found myself saying the Lord's Prayer. As I did so, her lips began to move and she joined in with me very faintly: 'Our Father who art in heaven, hallowed be thy name …' I was touched at a deep level. It had seemed such an impossible situation, but God was able to assure Mrs Lawrence that she was not alone and not forgotten.

Revd Robert Gillion

✢ ✢ ✢

How can a busy mother, with two or three screaming children, and a house to run, really be expected to think of God in the mayhem that is daily living?

The Sikh Gurus gave the answer to this important question in a beautiful verse in our Holy Book.

A boy gets paper, makes a kite
He flies it high in the air
And, though still talking
In an excited way with friends,
Always keeps his mind on the kite.

When a child is asleep in the cradle,
Inside and outside the house
Its mother is busy with various tasks
But she keeps her mind on the child.

The verse reminds us that we can, and should, keep our real priorities in mind at all times whatever else we may be doing.

Indarjit Singh

✤ ✤ ✤

What we place at the centre of our life matters. It shows us what is our deepest desire. The makers of prayer tell us that is where we will have to start our search for God.

He is not at the limits of our understanding but there in the midst of what is most important to us.

Mother Teresa used to tell a story. She said if you asked children in the west 'Where's God?' they'd point into the sky. If you asked children in India, they'd point at themselves … and then that remarkable woman would ask, 'And where do you point?'

Revd John Rackley

✢ ✢ ✢

In reality, God is the Cause of causes; rain does not come by itself. It is sent. Life is given; grain and food are provided. It is God who is the Sender of rain, the Giver of life and the Provider of sustenance. The Qur'an says: 'Adore not the sun or the moon but adore he who created them.'

Yusuf Islam

✢ ✢ ✢

There's nothing automatic about our spiritual life. Growth there is the result of effort: reading and thinking and praying.

Captain Charles King

✤ ✤ ✤

I've been thinking about health and
    fitness,
I was in a newsagent's yesterday
    getting the paper
and just stopped and stared at all
    the magazines
that are produced on health and
    fitness, and diets,
various exercise plans
for a beautiful and healthy body.

But I think we can do better
    than that.

This morning I would like to offer
you a regime for health
that not only benefits the body but
    actually exercises,
tones, sculpts, strengthens your
    feelings and thoughts.
I am talking about taking charge of
    developing a healthy mind.

If you wish to develop a healthy
    mind,
one of the sets of muscles you have to
    turn your mind to are those in
    your mouth.

You see the Buddha, who is often
    described
as a medicine for the illnesses of
humanity,

taught that we actually create a lot of
  illness
for ourselves and others through our
  day-to-day speech.

A poisonous tongue infects the
  speaker
as well as the person spoken to.

Words spoken or heard can burn in
  our hearts and minds
for days maybe even years eating us
  up.

And in the same kind
soothing words of appreciation,
of kindliness perfume the air;
they nourish and strength
all who are touched by their
  fragrance.

It is always easier to see faults
in others and ourselves,
so to counteract this
today's exercise for your mental
    health and sanity
is to try and rejoice in another's
    merits,
try to tell one person something you
    appreciate about them.

It can't fail to make you and the world
    a little bit brighter.

Dharmachari Nagaraja

✣ ✣ ✣

Wherever hungry people are fed, homeless people sheltered, rejected people welcomed, powerless people empowered, Christ is born again and all heaven breaks loose.

Revd Ruth Scott

✢ ✢ ✢

A surgeon once had an argument with his gardener about religion. 'I've cut into hundreds of bodies,' said the doctor, 'and I've never seen a human soul.'

'Well,' said the gardener, 'if you had cut into a tulip bulb, you wouldn't have seen a flower.'

Captain Charles King

✢ ✢ ✢

Everyone we meet, everything we do, every word we speak, every single moment of our lives is important. And each one of us counts for something – to others, to ourselves and for sure to God.

I love very much a saying of a medieval Spanish Jew, Bachya ibn Pakuda, that helps me get more out of life and put more in. He said: 'Days are like scrolls: write on them what you want to be remembered.'

Angela Wood

✢ ✢ ✢

St Paul encouraged the first Christians to live in order to grow to be like Jesus Christ. That kind of a life is no pretence – no impression – but the expression of what, through the gift of God, we really have become.

Revd John Newbury

✛ ✛ ✛

We who are Christians sometimes appear arrogant because we believe there is only one answer, and we have it. The truth is that God has given us – like the birds – a song to sing. And we shouldn't be afraid, or embarrassed, to sing it.

Captain Charles King

✛ ✛ ✛

As a Muslim, I am advised by my own tradition that to feel that Islam alone is true – whatever that means – is to show bad manners, as it were, to God, who leaves not a single person without loving guidance.

Faris Badawi

✢ ✢ ✢

What actually is God's religion? Is he Christian, Muslim, Hindu, Jewish or whatever? I don't think so. The Bhagavad-gita suggests that God's religion – and indeed the religion of the soul – is pure, unconditional love. It explains how we are all spirit souls, different from our bodies and their temporary designations. Religion, it says, is a process by which the soul awakens his or her eternal love for the Lord.

Krishna Dharma

✢ ✢ ✢

A Russian Orthodox friend once described an icon to me as a picture through which you catch a glimpse of a deeper reality. In other words, if you gaze at a real icon long enough it can have a spiritual effect upon you. I once met a young Frenchman who had been deeply influenced by an icon. He was a photographer who some years ago went on a journey to Russia. Russia in those days was a totally atheistic state and that suited the young man because he himself was an atheist. He told me he dismissed all religion as superstitious nonsense. But in Moscow he met an old woman who gave him a small icon of the Virgin Mary.

He admired the way it had been painted and when he got back to Paris he hung it on the wall of his flat. And then a strange thing happened. That icon began to haunt him. Its face seemed to speak of a far deeper reality than all the other pin-ups on his wall, and he wanted to know more about how it had been painted to have such a penetrating gaze. So he went out to one of the monasteries on Mount Athos in Greece to study the art of painting icons. The monks showed him that it was all a work of prayer and that every brush stroke was an act of worship. It completely bowled the young man over and he decided not only to become a painter of icons but also to become a monk himself. The icon had led him into a deeper spiritual reality.

Dr Pauline Webb

✣ ✣ ✣

The Sikh Gurus remind us that all our religious paintings, sculptures and similar devices are nothing more than the ornate covering of wonderful guidebooks on life. Of no use unless we open the covers and look within.

Indarjit Singh

✤ ✤ ✤

Once a rabbi noticed a shoemaker working far into the night. When asked why he was working so late, the shoemaker replied, 'For as long as the lamp is burning, we must do the repairs.' For the rest of his life, Rabbi Salanter used to repeat the words of the shoemaker as the most powerful reminder he knew for him to try constantly to make the most of his life, 'for as long as the lamp is burning, we must do the repairs'.

Because the world is sure in need of our help.

Rabbi Jackie Tabick

✢ ✢ ✢

Faith is an invitation to a life of exploration and the occasional identity-crisis.

Revd John Rackley

✢ ✢ ✢

My Christian faith is relevant to every item in the news. Because Christianity is about attitudes. Loving your neighbour. Loving your enemy. Turning the other cheek. Going the extra mile. Forgiving, not once, but seventy times seven times.

Captain Charles King

✢ ✢ ✢

I remember hearing of a missionary nun once who was going out to work among the poor in Calcutta. She was asked, 'Can you speak their language?'

'Well', she said, 'I shall learn it, but I already know five languages – the language of smiling, the language of weeping, the language of listening, the language of touching, and the language of loving.'

They are languages we all know, and could try speaking more often with the many strangers who have come to live among us now.

Dr Pauline Webb

✛ ✛ ✛

No wonder faith is always nudging us towards the view that putting people before products is always likely to be more productive in the end.

Revd Joel Edwards

✤ ✤ ✤

If you get the choice of sitting it out and looking at life, or dancing your way through it, I hope you dance!

Fr Brian D'Arcy

✤ ✤ ✤

'Life is a journey, travel it well,' says a current advertising campaign for heaven-knows-what. A lot of people regard life as a journey. But I read this the other day: 'We're not human beings on a spiritual journey. We're spiritual beings on a human journey.' I think the subtle difference between those two points of view actually gets to the meaning of life.

Captain Charles King

✣ ✣ ✣

It was Guru Nanak, the founder of Sikhism, who reminded us that God is not the least impressed by national or religious identity. It's how we respect and behave to our neighbour that really counts.

Indarjit Singh

✣ ✣ ✣

God alerts us to the fact that we can only call ourselves truly human when we've learnt to be compassionate with one another.

Oliver McTernan

✢ ✢ ✢

To me the only really effective missionary is the one who draws people to their belief by the way they behave and not by threats or bribes. Jesus didn't force anyone to believe in him – they were attracted to him by the person he was and is.

Canon Roger Royle

✢ ✢ ✢

Some travellers from Europe were going through heavy jungle with a local guide. He plunged ahead of them, hacking out a path. They got increasingly nervous. They could see no track, no signs. They began to grumble and complain, to query his skills. Finally, in exasperation he turned on them. 'You want to know where the path is? You want to know where you're going? Follow me, I am the path.'

Revd John Rackley

✣ ✣ ✣

I have just had the great privilege of visiting the Vatican and meeting the Pope. I engaged in debate with some of his staff on the subject of interfaith dialogue, and it has reminded me once again how much I hate the word 'tolerance'. It has such negative connotations. I mean, I tolerate the awfully loud music that sometimes emerges from our teenage children's bedrooms, because I love them, but I really can't understand what they find enjoyable in the awful cacophony of sound that surrounds them. That's toleration for you. But I hate it when I hear it said that interfaith dialogue takes place so that we can learn to tolerate each other. We have surely travelled further down the road than mere toleration.

Hopefully, we can now learn to appreciate each other's path to God. It reminds me of a traditional Jewish teaching. We are told that when a king of flesh and blood mints coins, they are all made bearing his image, and they are all boringly the same. But when the King of Kings, the Holy One – blessed be he – makes us, he also mints us all in his image, but we all turn out as unique individuals. So let us rejoice in the differences that God has himself created, accept that as God is so much greater than us there must be many ways to find him, and acknowledge the validity of the paths that others choose for themselves.

Rabbi Jackie Tabick

✜ ✜ ✜

If we choose to dwell on hatred, it grows ... and it leads to suffering, for ourselves and for those around us. If we dwell on positive feelings, they grow ... and they lead to happiness, for ourselves and for those around us.

Dharmachari Nagaraja

✜ ✜ ✜

Cricket is more than a game; it's almost a religion. We can think of the all-pervading nature of God in cricketing terms:

> I am the batsman and the bat;
> the bowler and the ball;
> The cricket pitch, stumps and all.

We talk of playing life with a straight bat – a reminder of correctness of action; we are told to keep our eyes on the ball, a reminder that we should not be diverted from our true objectives. From cricket we learn to play the game: that is, to be fair and honest in our dealings with others. If we live our lives in the spirit of these teachings of cricket, we can't go far wrong.

Indarjit Singh

✥ ✥ ✥

I've noticed in the last two weeks that virtually everyone who rings me up begins the conversation with an apology. 'I'm sorry to interrupt you. I expect you're watching the World Cup.' Though yesterday there was a slight change of emphasis: 'Roy, I'm sorry to take you away from the telly, I expect you're watching Wimbledon.' And only this morning my wife asked me what time the World Cup matches were being played today so that she could decide when to go to the supermarket. Apparently the local supermarket isn't so crowded when there's a game on. It seems that sport of every kind is dominating the consciousness of the whole population. Some are delighted about that while others deplore it. So I'm bound to upset someone this morning!

Now, as a lover of sport I would be the last to complain about the amount of coverage it gets. Throughout my lifetime I've played a variety of competitive sports and paid for the privilege of shouting advice if not abuse at my local football team. But as a society we may be in danger today of developing an obsession with sport. When one aspect of life predominates to the exclusion or detriment of others, things can get distorted – and I would include religion as well as sport in this category. Competition in sport is healthy until it assumes life and death proportions. Then it becomes destructive – with the end result of either physical or verbal violence. Who would have thought, for instance, that golf would have produced the kind of abuse directed at Colin Montgomery in the recent US Open?

Sport provides a livelihood for many and pleasure for millions more, so I hope that it will continue to flourish in our society. But I also hope that we will keep it in proportion. It is, after all, only a game. Only a part of the fabric of a society which needs the physical, mental, social and spiritual balance for its true health and wholeness.

Rt Revd Roy Williamson

✤ ✤ ✤

At an appraisal meeting, when asked what I thought was lacking in my life, I replied by saying that I needed to play more. The next time you see children at play, pause, and watch how caught up they are in the moment – living it fully.

An anonymous writer once said, 'We do not stop playing because we are old; we have grown old because we have stopped playing.' I shall definitely be playing more.

Revd Rose Hudson-Wilkin

✤ ✤ ✤

There's a Chinese proverb which says: 'Dig a well before you're thirsty.' If we're to have the spiritual resources to cope in a crisis we need to work at it before the crisis happens. Reading the right sort of books helps, prayer (any sort that works for you) is vital, and – as a million churchgoers would testify (and that's more people than go to watch football matches every weekend) – sharing together in worship can deepen faith.

. Captain Charles King

✢ ✢ ✢

Dreaming is not limited to the unreal. Dreaming is stretching the real beyond the limits of the present. Dreaming is not being bound by the merely possible.

Rabbi Jackie Tabick

✢ ✢ ✢

The answer to life's questions lies inside you. All you need to do is to look, to listen and to trust your inner voice.

Fr Brian D'Arcy

✤ ✤ ✤

Yesterday's wisdom can be today's path to new horizons. We do have to learn for ourselves but not as if no one's been there before us.

Revd John Rackley

✤ ✤ ✤

Sometimes we think that world leaders are a breed apart without human feelings. As the saying goes – power corrupts, absolute power corrupts absolutely.

That was why it was interesting to read

about Kofi Annan, the UN Secretary-General who was awarded the Noble Peace Prize. Two of his greatest virtues are his compassion and his faith. Apparently his compassion frightens other political leaders. They claim that his warm heart is praiseworthy at an individual level, but would be disastrous if transferred to global politics. Which says more about political standards than it does about the Secretary-General.

Seasoned journalists recall how Kofi Annan always seems to pick out individuals, in the midst of disasters. In East Timor he sat on the side of the road with a man who burst into tears recounting the things which had happened to him. And in Kosovo he sat with a one-hundred-year-old woman who could only say over and over again, 'How could this happen to me at my age?'

The basis of his compassion is his faith.

Early in the morning as he lies in bed he prays. Sometimes he's quoted as saying, 'I ask questions in my prayers. The world is so cruel. How can people be so heartless? What can one do?' And he goes on, 'I still struggle with evil, I don't understand how there can be so much of it in the world. You look at its impact and you see young people who have no hope. They are destroyed.'

He has a tree in his backyard which he calls his Thinking Tree. There he meditates about how to bring hope to the victims of violence and sanity to the world's crises.

At such times it's easy to see how his compassion could be laughed at, how his faith would be tested and why his meditation tree is probably his most effective weapon in maintaining world peace.

Kofi Annan has an unenviable job. Perhaps his philosophy is best summed up in St

Matthew's Gospel: 'I am sending you out like sheep among wolves. Be as cunning as serpents and as innocent as a dove.' A tough task for him and for us.

Fr Brian D'Arcy

✛ ✛ ✛

When the Beatles' song 'Let it be' first came out, I hated it, though I was – and still am – a great Beatles fan. Letting anything be was the opposite of what I thought life was saying, of what I wanted to say about life. There were protests to be made, issues to stand up for, wrongs to be righted and all kinds of dragons to be slain. Letting things be would be soft and silly. It would mean you didn't care or you'd given up. Perhaps I didn't understand the song or perhaps I had a lot more growing up – and growing 'in' – to do. Perhaps I have grown soft and silly, but I prefer to think of it as mellowing – and myself as just a late developer! Now it means feeling comfortable with who I am, and loving the world as it really is, as well as as it should be. And that's how God loves.

Angela Wood

✣ ✣ ✣

Our society is like a shop window in which someone has swapped all the price tags around. The things of true value have been marked down as almost worthless, and the tat is venerated.

Captain Charles King

✣ ✣ ✣

I remember a saying my father put in my autograph book when I was a child. 'You were born an original. Don't become a copy.'

Dr Pauline Webb

✠ ✠ ✠

We should never underestimate the power of a simple action. Good, like evil, always has a ripple effect. Your act of kindness today may well influence someone to an act of heroism which in turn could change the world. Never underestimate the power of a simple good act.

Fr Brian D'Arcy

✠ ✠ ✠

The very last thing I want to do is appear rude, but I am in a bit of a hurry. You see, I have to be at a school near the Elephant and Castle by 10.10 to do an assembly – and I mustn't be late. The head teacher Mrs Owens likes to begin on time with the children all sitting quietly, up straight and eagerly expectant. Mrs Posnor will be poised at the piano: she has transformed the singing in that school. The words have always been good – but then you would expect that from a school named after Charles Dickens – but Mrs Posnor has now got them singing their hearts out.

So when I leave, there is always a spring in my step and happiness in my heart. But there is also a certain element of doubt in my head. For the past few years, schools have been under tremendous pressure to deliver the goods. All the political parties have education high on their manifesto agendas. But I am concerned that schools are now being asked to teach things that should be taught at home. Schools are also expected to set standards that are no longer accepted or at least followed by the rest of society. At a very early age many of our children are subjected to double standards. It's no wonder they're confused.

Any child found misbehaving this morning will be quietly taken to sit at their teacher's side – and yet those same children have only got to turn on the telly or look at the papers and they will often see adults behaving very badly.

All faiths put tremendous emphasis on the care of children – they are not being properly cared for when they are taught one thing in school but life gives them a totally different message.

Canon Roger Royle

✢ ✢ ✢

In ancient times, two rabbis went to view the cities in the land of Israel. In every one they visited they asked to see the guardians of the city. First the bankers and merchants were brought out. 'No, not them!' Then out came the police officers and politicians. 'Certainly not them!'

Finally, in desperation, the people said, 'Who d'you want, then?' And they said, 'The teachers … we want to see the teachers. They're the guardians of the city.'

Angela Wood

✣ ✣ ✣

One of the most striking things I've noticed is that many young and very old people say similar things A man very close to death once said to me, 'You know, I feel that at the end of my life I can say that all that really matters in life is relationships and how you treat people, all that is really important is that you have a good heart and love others.' Teenagers have said the same thing to me, and what is so worrying about our society is that we dismiss the opinions of both of these groups. We dump the old and forget about them and we often feel a kind of punitive rage against the young for their impertinent opinions. Let's not wait until we are at the very end of our lives to relearn things that we intuitively felt when we were young.

Faris Badawi

✢ ✢ ✢

A little boy was put to bed one night and within an hour his mum heard a great crash. He'd fallen out of bed. Comforting him, she asked why it had happened.

'I guess I didn't move away from where I got in,' he said. A child wise beyond his years.

It happens so often – in our faith, our understanding of people, developing a skill – we never get beyond where we first started, we never move on. Move on from that childish picture of God; that experience of adults in our early years; the first piano lesson – or whatever.

Revd John Rackley

✧ ✧ ✧

A failure that we learn from is not a failure at all.

Fr Brian D'Arcy

✢ ✢ ✢

Just recently I was giving the Last Rites to a lovely ninety-year-old woman. She was at home, in her own bed, surrounded by her family. She appeared to be in a coma but just at the moment when I prayed, 'Go forth, Christian soul …' she opened her eyes and said in a loud voice, 'Do I owe you any money?' and with that she died. Her generation, of course, didn't get into debt.

And then there was Toots, ninety-five years old and the life and soul of any and every party. I visited her in hospital shortly before she died. My hands were cold. As soon as Toots felt them, she threw her blankets back, saying, 'You get in here with me, love, and I'll soon warm you up!'

Or wonderful Basil Knightly, another ninety-five-year-old who died just last week. Again I was at his bedside, his family round him. He joined in all the prayers, and as I pronounced the final blessing he asked, 'Was that my funeral service?'

'No, Basil, it wasn't,' I said, 'because you're not dead yet.'

'In that case,' he replied, 'I hope you've brought me something to eat.' He died a few hours later after a cup of tea and two biscuits.

Just three examples of the triumph of the human spirit that the older generation can show us. I salute them.

Revd Murray Grant

✢ ✢ ✢

At exam time it is good to remember that there is more to life than passing exams.

To make the point: at a college in America, a professor on the first day of class challenged each of the freshers to get to know someone they didn't know already. One student got a gentle touch on the shoulder, and when she turned around there was a little old lady beaming up at her with a smile that lit up the room.

'My name is Rose and I am eighty-seven years old. May I give you a hug?' she said.

The young student laughed and asked the old lady why she was at college.

'One reason I am here is to meet a rich husband, get married, have a couple of children. But if you want the serious answer it's because I always dreamed of having a college education and now I'm getting one,' she replied.

The two became firm friends. Over the

year Rose became a campus icon. At the end of the semester they invited her to speak to the class.

'I've learned a few secrets to staying young, being happy and achieving success,' she began. 'You have to laugh and find humour every day.

'You've got to have a dream. When you lose your dreams you die. So many people are walking around dead and don't even know it.

'There is huge difference between growing older and growing up. Anybody can grow older. The trick is to grow up by always finding the opportunity to change.

'The elderly usually don't have regrets for what we did, but rather for the things we did not do. The only people who fear death are those with regrets.'

Rose finished her degree and graduated when she was eighty-eight years old. One week after her graduation Rose died peacefully in her sleep. Over two thousand students attended her funeral in tribute to the wonderful woman who taught by example that it is never too late to be all you can possibly be. On her order of service was this quote: 'Growing older is mandatory. Growing up is optional.'

Fr Brian D'Arcy

✤ ✤ ✤

This is an age-old recipe but it's a real classic. You'll need one pair of un-blinkered eyes – the sort that aren't blinded by bigotry and prejudice. One pair of listening ears. One mouth big enough to speak out against injustice, but small enough to stop you putting a foot in it. One determined chin. One nose for adventure. A pair of broad shoulders that can carry the rough with the smooth. One chest, or as Sarah Kennedy says, one pair of chesticles, full of the milk of human kindness. One belly – it's essential you get the kind that's good for laughing. One bottom that won't sit down on the job in hand.

Two arms – you'll need the variety that are better at reaching out to others than clutching everything to themselves. One pair of hands with a gentle touch. Two legs that can walk the extra mile for friend and stranger. A pair of feet that will tread carefully through someone else's sacred space.

Stir everything up with a little liquid courage, making sure you don't beat in a lot of hot air.

Then add two crucial ingredients that complement each other very well – an intelligent brain and a big heart. I understand female brains are much cheaper than their male counterparts. Apparently this is because used items always cost less. If you can't find a good brain, don't worry, but don't settle for anything less than the best when it comes to the heart. A fool with a heart is often a great asset, whereas a heartless bright spark is a walking disaster.

Finally, don't forget the condiments. They add a good bit of spice to life, but must be used with care and sensitivity otherwise they'll ruin the recipe.

Mix everything together with love, making sure it's not the cheap kind that's full of artificial additives. The costly variety is well worth the price because it can turn even the most disastrous ingredients into a recipe fit for a king. Simmer gently for as long as it takes to produce a half-decent human being.

It's not an easy recipe but it's well worth the effort.

Revd Ruth Scott

✢ ✢ ✢

I have a theory that age doesn't matter. It's attitude that's important. The oldest member of one of my congregations was a hundred and one. She had a zest for life, was alert and quick-witted, and had the most lovely, unlined face. One day she said to me that she wanted to buy a new coat for winter. 'But I want a good one,' she said. 'Because I want it to last!'

Revd Paul Hulme

✛ ✛ ✛

There used to be an old hymn that asked the question 'Is it well with your soul?' And I reckon that's the most important question of all if we're to be really healthy.

For an MOT for the soul I suggest just three tests:

1 How often do we say 'Thank you' – not just to other people (though I think we ought to show our gratitude to others far more often than we do) but thanks to the One who is the very source of our life, the God who gives us the precious gift of each new day?

2 How often do we say 'Sorry' – again, not just to anyone whom we've wronged in some way or other, but sorry to God, who knows even our secret faults?

3 And most important of all, how often do we give ourselves a few moments each day just to be quiet and relaxed in God's presence and to be reassured by the message of God's love and forgiveness?

Dr Pauline Webb

✢ ✢ ✢

The Old Testament declares that where there is no vision the people fall apart.

We need visionaries. Dreamers. People who are not hampered by their past, but who let it feed their hope for the future. They choose from the past the best and the good. They look ahead, resourced by what they remember.

So, paradoxically, the best dreamers are people with a past – not the young.

The Old Testament declares, 'When the spirit of God works … Your young may see visions, but it is the old men who dream dreams.'

Revd John Rackley

✜ ✜ ✜

So it is best not to get too discouraged about our life. Keep struggling, keep trying. Enjoy the happiness God sends. Nothing is wasted and all shall be well.

Fr Brian D'Arcy

✤ ✤ ✤

Humility means nothing more than complete honesty about ourselves, our strengths as well as our weaknesses. It includes a mature self-belief that, being made in the image of God, we have a valuable contribution to make to the life of our family, our friends and our community. We weren't created to be doormats, but ladders that reach upwards and help others to do the same.

Rt Revd Roy Williamson

✤ ✤ ✤

I quite like the idea of New Year resolutions. They can be just the kick in the pants we sometimes need. But they need to be challenging. Not like the man who took up archery but couldn't get the hang of it. So to impress his neighbours he fired his arrows in the general direction of his wooden garage door, then painted targets round the arrows wherever they landed, giving the impression that each one had hit the bull's-eye. Sometimes, I fear, we do much the same with the targets we set ourselves in life – settling too often for the easy option, the low standard …

Jesus said he came to bring us life in all its fullness. Anyone who's still looking for a challenging New Year resolution might like to decide to spend some time discovering just what he meant by that.

Captain Charles King

✤ ✤ ✤

For a lot of people, Christmas is not a good time. If you're lonely, depressed, things going wrong, it's all much worse at Christmastime. You imagine that everyone else is having a good time except you. I had that experience when I was a teenager. I had fallen out with my parents, joined the Merchant Navy and gone to sea. After trips on tankers and cargo boats, and a terrifying one on a small coaster that nearly sank in a storm, I got a job washing dishes on the *Queen Mary*.

It may have been glamorous for the passengers but certainly not for us. We, the lowest form of shipboard life, washed dishes from seven in the morning until eleven at night – with three half-hours off for meals. When we got fed up we threw piles of greasy dishes through the porthole. The undersea route to New York must be paved with plates!

One night, I went up on deck feeling depressed. I was estranged from my family, and very, very lonely.

And it was near Christmas.

The Atlantic seemed immense and the *Queen Mary*, which had seemed so huge tied up in Southampton, was very small in all that sea and space. The sky, stretching from horizon to horizon, was spangled with millions of stars.

I have never ever felt so lonely, so small, so insignificant, in my life. Looking back on that experience I know now that it was one of the richest of my life. It was the start of my spiritual journey. A journey to find out who I was, whether I mattered, what the point was of anything. And who was responsible for it all, anyway.

In those days I wasn't a believer, but I did read the Bible and later discovered Psalm 8:

When I consider thy heavens,
the work of thy fingers,

the moon and the stars,
which thou hast ordained;

what is man …?

That was the experience that I had had on
deck of the *Queen Mary* that cold, starlit
December night. What is man? But the psalm
goes on to say,

what is man, that thou art
mindful of him?
and the son of man, that thou
visitest him?

That was what I had to find out. And I have.
That God cares for me. And for every one of
you.

And that is the wonderful message of Christmas.

Revd Murray Grant

✜ ✜ ✜

When I first crossed the Irish Sea to work in London as a lay missionary, I spent most of my days on the streets around Southwark Cathedral, knocking on doors and trying to help people in need. There's one door in particular I remember to this day, because of the words written just above the letter-box: they read 'Bring good news – and knock loudly.'

Rt Revd Roy Williamson

✜ ✜ ✜

Jesus, though he never condemned people for being rich, did warn that it could be a riskier business than the stock market, because wealth only sharpens the questions that all of us have to answer. What have I done with what I've received? However little that might be, I still have to answer for it before the God whose way is about giving and sharing and using what I have for the good of others. And what really comes first in my life? Is it holding on to what I've got and busting a gut to get more? Or is it about putting what God wants before everything, and trusting him to see me through?

Revd Roy Jenkins

✤ ✤ ✤

The end of Lent is in sight. Palm Sunday next weekend, then Holy Week.

A time of prayer for Christians, when we

decide what really matters to us. I've been drawing on my memories of Israel.

Lent recalls the Temptation of Jesus in the wilderness. When I was there I found the place awesome. I was brought up in the green rolling hills of Devon. It was a shock to be in such a dry, dusty environment. What could live there? How could it be a place of prayer?

I was leading a pilgrimage. But on this occasion I let them go to look at yet another monastery and took off on my own.

I climbed a small hill. The heat was appalling. I thought of Jesus. Here he had wondered what sort of life would serve God. It was a time of turmoil for him. A place of wild beasts and angels, the Bible tells us.

How could that desert have helped him, I wondered.

Baked hard earth. Rocks twisted into harsh

shapes. It was disconcerting. I longed for a lush Devon valley.

Then I noticed something. Gradually I was aware that the air was full of a heady, herbal scent. And there at my feet, caked in dust, were tiny bushes not unlike the heather of Dartmoor. A fragrance came from them.

The heat and dust were transformed.

I saw it all differently.

The place had a kindness I had not imagined.

Balance was restored.

As Jesus discovered, so had I – the God of beauty and purpose was not absent, even in the wilderness.

Wild beasts and angels. Wild beasts and angels.

Revd John Rackley

✠ ✠ ✠

At the beginning of Holy Week forgiveness is a good theme to look at. Gandhi remembers that at fifteen he stole a piece of gold from his brother. But then he felt so bad about it that he had to confess it to his father. He wrote the sin on a piece of paper, asking for forgiveness and punishment, and promised never to steal again.

His father was sick at the time and Gandhi handed him the note by the bedside, waiting for judgement. His father sat up in bed and read the note. As he read it tears came to his eyes, and instead of getting angry the father hugged the repentant son and that was the end of the matter. The experience of being loved while still in sin, as it were, had a profound effect on Gandhi. And he said later, 'Only the person who has experienced this kind of love can know the effect of it.'

Fr Brian D'Arcy

✥ ✥ ✥

Talking and listening carefully is vitally important in something like peace negotiations. And on a general level, caring for people includes, among other things, genuine listening. Listening properly requires time, concentration and practice if any answer is to be worthwhile.

Those who pray believe they speak to God who listens – really listens – to them, and who hears and is concerned about what they say. That belief is expressed at the end of many prayers in the phrase: 'The Lord hears our prayer. Thanks be to God.'

Revd John Newbury

✤ ✤ ✤

Can you remember, the last time you asked someone how they were doing, what the response was? 'Hi! How are you?'

The usual response coming back is, 'Not too bad.' My bishop in Jamaica once said to a lady who gave him that reply, 'But I'm not accusing you of anything.'

The negativity by which we surround ourselves is due, I believe, to the poor images we have of ourselves. We have difficulty understanding the good others see in us. When someone gives us a compliment, we are quick to point out what is wrong. When someone supports or encourages us, we remind them of our failures.

When you don't feel good about yourself, it is hard to feel good about anything or anyone else. You miss the value and worth of every experience. You limit yourself because you don't feel good about who you are or what you do. This path eventually leads to self-destruction.

The only way to get out of this vicious cycle is to begin to believe in ourselves.

Nelson Mandela captured it well when he said, 'You are a child of God. Your playing small doesn't serve the world. There's nothing enlightened about shrinking so that other people won't feel insecure around you. We are all meant to shine, as children do. We are born to make manifest the glory of God that is within us. It's not just in some of us, it's in everyone.' He continues to say that 'as we let our own light shine, we consciously give other people permission to do the same'.

Don't wait, therefore, for someone to tell you how wonderful you are. Just simply believe it, know it! Look deep within yourself. As we get to know and affirm ourselves for who we are, we become aware of the divinity that we share. What better place to find God than within ourselves.

Revd Rose Hudson-Wilkin

✣ ✣ ✣

Palm Cross – to help us ponder the meaning of Good Friday.

Martin Luther King died thirty years ago. I was a student preparing for the Baptist ministry. I can still remember the effect of his assassination on me. He too was a Baptist. He was deeply committed to civil rights. He was a great preacher. People were inspired to change.

Thirty years on I find time hasn't served him well. His legacy is troubled, his reputation questioned. Yet for a while his words invigorated and re-ennobled his people.

Here are some of them:

> To our most bitter opponents we say, 'We shall match your capacity to inflict suffering by our capacity to endure suffering. Non-cooperation with evil is as much an obligation as cooperation with good. One day we

shall win freedom and not only for ourselves.

I find those words deeply moving. Not because he said them but because they speak of a way of life that we only occasionally glimpse.

But the glimpses are exciting. In families torn apart by anger, in places like Northern Ireland and Israel, there are people living not in hatred but in defiant hope. They accept awkwardness, harshness and death and do not let the violence control them.

Like the man on the cross they accept the suffering for the joy that is to come.

May their patience be rewarded.

Revd John Rackley

✥ ✥ ✥

One day an expert in time management was speaking to a group of business students and, to emphasise a point, used an example they will never forget.

Standing in front of this group of high achievers he said, 'Let's carry out a little experiment.' Then he pulled out a one-gallon, wide-mouthed preserving jar and sat it on the table in front of him. Next he produced about a dozen hand-sized rocks and carefully placed them, one at a time, in the jar. When the jar was filled to the top and no more rocks would fit inside he asked, 'Is this jar full?'

Everyone in the class said, 'Yes.'

'Really?' He reached under the table and pulled out a bucket of gravel. Then he dumped some gravel in and shook the jar so that the gravel worked its way down into the spaces between the rocks. Then he asked the group once more, 'Is this jar full?'

By this time the class was on to him and agreed that it probably wasn't.

So he reached under the table again and this time brought out a bucket of sand. He dumped the sand in the jar and it went into all the spaces between the rocks and the gravel. Once more the question, 'Is the jar full?'

'No!' the class shouted. And they were right.

Then he grabbed a jug of water and began to pour it in until the jar was fill to the brim. He looked at the class and asked, 'What's the point of this experiment?'

One eager student interpreted it his way. 'The point is, no matter how full your schedule is, if you try really hard you can always fit some more things into it.'

'No,' the speaker replied. 'That's not the point. The truth this illustration teaches is this. If you don't put the big rocks in first you'll never get them in at all.'

So the question you have to ask yourself today is this: 'What are the "big rocks" in your life?' Your children? Your loved ones? Your education? Your dreams? Your charitable work? Doing the things you love? Time for yourself? Your health? Your spouse or your partner?

Whatever it is, remember to put these big rocks in first or you will never get them in at all. In American jargon, if you sweat the little stuff then you will fill your life with little things to worry about but which really don't matter, and you will never have the real quality time you need to spend on the important issues.

So as you start the day take a little time out to reflect on this parable. Decide what is really important in your life, then decide how much of it you can get done today. And finally start off doing it right now. All the other incidentals can be fitted in later, and if they are never fitted in you will never be any worse off.

Fr Brian D'Arcy

✢ ✢ ✢

One of the great things about the Christian faith is the way our Creator seems to be willing to entrust his plans to imperfect people. Look at the twelve disciples. Two of them were forever arguing, one denied Jesus, one doubted him, one was so thick he never did get the point ('Have I been so long with you and still you don't understand?' said Jesus) and most of the others were so ordinary that when Matthew, Mark, Luke and John wrote the Gospels they couldn't think of a single interesting thing to say about them. And yet God chose them, and trusted them to do his work.

Captain Charles King

✤ ✤ ✤

No matter how fierce the opposition, the light of true religion can never be extinguished.

Fidelma Meehan

✤ ✤ ✤

The first official fatality in the World Trade Center disaster was a Franciscan priest, Fr Mychal Judge, who was chaplain to the New York Fire Department. The sixty-eight-year-old priest was a respected figure in New York who helped run a soup kitchen, ministered to AIDS patients, and officiated at countless baptisms, weddings and funerals in addition to his work with the fire-fighters.

At his funeral, his friend Fr Michael Dufly spoke of the moment of his death.

'Look how Fr Mychal died,' he said. 'He was right there where the action was, and that's where he always wanted to be. He was praying with a dying man. He was talking to God and he was helping someone in need. Can you honestly think of a better way to die?'

Fr Brian D'Arcy

✣ ✣ ✣

Probably we've all encountered the teacher who said no one deserved an 'A' or a boss who never said, 'Well done.'

Why do we wait to serve the wine? Jesus never reached the age of forty. Perhaps

knowing he wouldn't be here long is what
caused him to serve the best wine first.

✥ ✥ ✥

Tapping into real life still has an edge on
the computer keyboard.

Indarjit Singh

✥ ✥ ✥

A woman phoned to say her computer had
gone completely dead – the screen had
blanked out on her. So the engineer patiently
asked her to check that it was plugged in
properly. Yes, she said, all the plugs were
switched on. So he asked her to see if the
monitor and computer were connected at the
back.

'I can't see round the back,' she said.

'Why not?' he asked.

'Because it's dark.'

'Well, put the light on,' he suggested.

'I can't,' she replied. 'There's been a power cut.'

Well, even I know that a computer can't work if there's no external power. However brilliant its internal mechanism may be, it still has to be switched on to an external source of energy, just like any of us. Some people seem to think they can get through life relying entirely on their own strength, but sooner or later everyone needs help from someone beyond themselves. It might be advice from a good friend, or some kind of support agency. But the best help of all comes from the central source of power, the God who first breathed life into us and who knows, as the psalmist puts it, how fearfully and wonderfully we are made. I believe that prayer is a way of switching on to that power, a personal way of communicating with God, as instant and immediate as an e-mail, which no one else can hack into.

Dr Pauline Webb

✜ ✜ ✜

I wonder if we deliberately seek out noise because we are afraid of being with ourselves? We also surround ourselves with physical as well as mental clutter. All this prevents us from being at peace with ourselves. Even if we all can't get away physically on this sabbatical, we all have the capacity to create an inner place of silence. A place where we can be at one with ourselves. When we perfect the art of silence, chances

are we will grow into better human beings –
at one with our Creator.

Revd Rose Hudson-Wilkin

✛ ✛ ✛

The real world is a world where things go wrong, a world where we have to get stuck in and get our hands dirty. A world where we can learn from the terrible mistakes we make.

Revd Murray Grant

✛ ✛ ✛

I'm feeling like a real vicar at the moment! I have had a baptism preparation on Monday, a funeral yesterday and a wedding today. So I thought about life! Well, you would, wouldn't you? When do you learn your earliest philosophy for life?

In my last parish we almost had as many children in our Sunday School as in the main service. So once I sent all the adults to Sunday School classes and the youngsters joined me for the service. It was such fun for the adults to experience the delights of storytelling, drawing and painting – and those who really wanted to regress spent time playing in the sand tray!

'Let the children come to me, for theirs is the kingdom of God,' said Jesus.

Sometimes our adult ways can get so complicated. There's a wonderful piece of writing by a fellow-minister, Robert Fulgham, who describes the kindergarten at Sunday School where he found wisdom.

- Share everything.

- Play fair.

- Don't hit people.

- Put things back where you found them.

- Clean up your own mess.

- Don't take things that are not yours.

- Say you're sorry when you hurt somebody.

- Wash your hands before you eat.

- Flush.

- Warm cookies and cold milk are good for you.

- Live a balanced life – learn some and think some and draw and paint and sing and dance and play and work every day some.

- Take a nap every afternoon.

- When you go out into the world, watch out for traffic, hold hands, and stick together.

- Be aware of wonder. Remember the little seed in the Styrofoam cup; the roots go down and the plant goes up and nobody really knows how or why, but we are all like that.

- Goldfish and hamsters and white mice and even the little seed in the Styrofoam cup – they all die. So do we.

- Remember the first word you learned from Janet and John books: 'Look!'

(From Robert Fulghum's book,
All I Really Need to Know I Learned in Kindergarten,
published by Grafton Books, 1989)

Think what a better world it would be if we all – the whole world – had cookies and milk about three o'clock every afternoon and then lay down on our blankies for a nap.

Or if all governments had a basic policy to always put things back where they found them and to clean up after their own mess. And it is still true, no matter how old you are – when you go out into the world, it is better to hold hands and stick together.

Revd Robert Gillion

✣ ✣ ✣

A story is told of a discontented king who was so anxious he couldn't sleep or even think straight. So he called his wise men together and asked them what he could do.

One very old and wise man said: 'Find a

man in your kingdom who is content, then wear his shirt for a day and a night, and you'll be content.'

That sounded like a good idea to the king, so he ordered his servants to search for such a man. Days merged into weeks before his servants returned. 'Well,' said the king, 'did you find a contented man?'

'Yes, sire,' said his servants.

'Where is his shirt, then?' asked the king.

'Your majesty,' came the reply, 'he didn't have one on!'

As the good book says, 'Godliness with contentment is great gain.'

Captain Charles King

✠ ✠ ✠

If in doubt, I believe a Christian attitude is to put the rights of others before our own.

Rt Revd Roy Williamson

✣ ✣ ✣

I visited a school recently and was shown round the art room. The children's work was on display. They had been asked to draw their house. So there were lots of gates and paths, front doors and roofs, TV aerials – except for one. This was the inside of the girl's playroom looking out through the window.

Now that's an original thinker at work. Long may she be like that.

Revd John Rackley

✣ ✣ ✣

I know that as a Christian I should be all sweetness and light. That's very difficult at times. None more so than when I am having my annual plant sale for Christian Aid in my garden. It was last Saturday.

It's a lot of work preparing for it – getting up at 5 a.m. for at least three mornings to go to New Covent Garden to buy the plants. I have no compunction in putting a heavy mark-up on them because of the cause. Anyway, I think Christian Aid Week is *the* time when Christians should put their money where their mouths are.

Some people think otherwise – usually the wealthier ones.

'You don't really expect me to pay one pound for this petunia, do you?'

'Yes, madam,' I reply, 'because I'm doing it for the hungry, the homeless, the sick, for people in parts of the world that haven't our advantages. For one measly pound, you get a petunia and they get hope. OK?'

If looks could kill, I should have dropped dead in my own herbaceous border.

Revd Murray Grant

✢ ✢ ✢

A man was tending his front garden when a neighbour congratulated him on how beautiful it looked. 'Isn't God wonderful?' said the neighbour.

'Hmm', said the man. 'You should have seen what this garden looked like when God had it to himself!'

The fact is that looking after our beautiful world is a partnership between the Creator and us, and it's good that more and more of us are accepting responsibility for this.

But I think there's a bigger truth here,

which is that we all have to take a measure of responsibility for our own lives. Faith in God is marvellous – you'd expect me to say that. Believing that God will sort everything out for us (on the 'Mother Nature' principle) is great – but we can't abdicate all responsibility.

What we have to do, it seems to me, is to try to find out what God's plan for our life is, and then play our part. And sometimes that might well involve getting the chainsaw out and hacking away at a few unhelpful things.

Captain Charles King

✢ ✢ ✢

Since Adam and Eve, we human beings have subconsciously and consciously dreamt of returning to that Garden from which we were expelled. However, unlike those who tediously concentrate on clearing the weeds of this world, believers in the hereafter are aiming for the real thing: the ultimate Garden experience. And it's possible. That's the good news which all the Prophets brought, but which many people have forgotten.

The Qur'an reminds us of this perfect abode and warns us of the opposite; it gives us a picture of this Paradise and speaks of those who are fit to live there; but for those too busy with this world it also speaks of the other place!

> The parable of the Garden which the righteous are promised!
>
> Beneath it flows rivers: Perpetual is the enjoyment thereof and the shade therein: Such is the end of the Righteous; and the end of Unbelievers is the Fire.
>
> Yusuf Islam

✢ ✢ ✢

The potential for human good is amazing. It makes the impossible happen, turns suffering into healing and despair to hope.

Fr Brian D'Arcy

✤ ✤ ✤

A couple of years ago, I bought a lightweight suit in the sales. It was a real bargain and the salesman said it fitted perfectly. Last month, when summer finally came and I was due to go to court – as a JP, I hasten to add – I thought I'd wear it and impress everyone.

To me the suit seemed a little loose, not quite the perfect fit that the salesman assured me. But then I'm not very good at these things. I showed it to my wife. Clearly she wasn't too impressed and her diplomatic comment that it really wasn't 'that bad' didn't exactly reassure. I went off to court feeling distinctly shabby. When I got back, my little grandson Simran was there. He eyed me curiously and asked, 'Is that your court costume?'

It was the word 'costume' that got me. Clearly I must have looked like a clown. I haven't worn the suit since.

It's a wonderful thing about children, this innocence of expression without the artificial diplomacy of adults. The difficult job for parents is to build on this earnestness and encourage children to develop an open and honest attitude to others, in a world in which cynicism and hypocrisy often seem to rule. But it's not all one way. Children have a lot to teach parents and grandparents, and are wonderful in cutting us down to size, as clowns or whatever.

Some five hundred years ago, Guru Nanak

reminded us of this importance of the family. In the India of that time, it was common for people to leave their families and go off to the wilderness in search of God. The Guru said, why on earth go to the wilderness when he is there in the challenges of ordinary family life? It's in the family that we learn about selfless love, and with the help of wife, husband and – particularly – children, see something of our own pretensions and inadequacies.

Indarjit Singh

✢ ✢ ✢

Aggression is deeply seated in our nature – but unless we are prepared to put some sort of check on ourselves we are going to create a world in which no one is safe. It's about time the peacemakers were given a chance, because in the end we are told that they are the ones who will be blessed.

Canon Roger Royle

✤ ✤ ✤

A second look might tell us something about Scripture and what it's trying to teach us: that good and evil are states of tension within each person. And that our battle is not necessarily outside us, but within us. The war of the self, not the war of the worlds.

Yusuf Islam

✤ ✤ ✤

At the heart of the Christian gospel is a promise from God that forgiveness is always possible, when repentance is shown.

As the Bible poetically puts it: 'Though your sins be as scarlet, they shall be white as snow.'

Captain Charles King

✤ ✤ ✤

Hate is not conquered by hate; hate is conquered by love. Those who realise this settle their quarrels peacefully.

Dharmachari Nagaraja

✤ ✤ ✤

Wherever barriers are found, they need to be replaced by bridges. Bridges are for walking across, for meeting and listening to one another. Hearing leads to understanding, and understanding can lead to respect.

Rt Revd Roy Williamson

✤ ✤ ✤

The Bible tells us that we are made in the 'image and likeness of God'. Living alongside and interacting with people of different races and beliefs has helped me to appreciate that the Bible is not talking about outward appearances. It is our human capacity to relate to others, to be compassionate and to love unconditionally that makes us Godlike.

Oliver McTernan

✢ ✢ ✢

In my own homeland of Northern Ireland, I'm amazed at how one Holy Book, based on love, can be interpreted in so many different ways to justify hatred.

Recently I saw a play about how the light of true religion becomes obscured by interpretations.

It was about a special lamp which guided

people. This lamp was so precious that everyone wanted to adorn it with their own beautiful cloth, until finally the lamp was totally hidden under layers of cloth and the people were left in darkness.

Fidelma Meehan

✣ ✣ ✣

I have recently emerged out of my reclusive corner to sing for a cause I believe in – Bosnia – which has suffered one of the most horrendous attempts of cold-blooded genocide in recent years.

Many of us who saw the horrors and tragedy of the war must have thought in the back of our minds that the root of this conflict lies with religion. Indeed! It's true to say that Bosnia stands on the fault line of East and West; it embraces the people of three major faiths: Islam, Christian Orthodoxy and Catholicism. But is it truly religion that is to blame? Could such atrocities really be committed by real people of faith? I think not!

It's true to say that some of the most savage massacres in the history of humanity took place in the 'name' of religion – but though some may claim that modern secularism has now been able to rise over the petty differences of religious fanaticism, it must be accepted that, in fact, some of the largest numbers of people ever to have been killed were those who died in world wars, fuelled not by religion but by violent nationalism. And as recently as only fifty years ago.

What does this mean? To me it means that no matter what name you give it, *intolerance*, be it religious or racial, is the root cause of the problem.

Many may not know that Islam embodies religious tolerance within its teaching. The only justification for fighting in Islam is to secure the people's right to worship God without fear, in peace and security – or to retaliate against aggression and attack. God specifies how Muslims should treat people of other faiths, and in the Qur'an it says:

Regarding those who do not fight you for your faith nor drive you out of your homes. God does not forbid you from dealing kindly and justly with them: for God loves those who are just. It is only regarding those who fight you for your faith, and drive you out of your homes and support others in driving you out, that God forbids you from turning to them for friendship and protection.

I do wish that more of us could learn the spirit of tolerance which religion is supposed to teach. People would then blame religion much less than they do now for the injustices that we see around us.

Humour is very much a two-edged sword. It can have a fierce cutting edge as well as being able to take the sting out of a situation.

Canon Roger Royle

✠ ✠ ✠

Just outside the United Nations building in New York is the statue of a man with a gun. The barrel of the gun is twisted into a knot, and underneath is the caption, 'Knot the gun'. A poor pun, but sound comment in a world awash with arms. There is something badly wrong when rich countries continue to make themselves richer by supplying weapons of destruction to the poor.

Better to get back to the old days of selling beads and cheap trinkets – sell anything! But, as we start a new millennium, it's high time we tied a huge knot in the international arms trade.

Indarjit Singh

✜ ✜ ✜

The best response we can give to human disasters is to offer help. When my life's gone adrift I've not wanted platitudes and clichés but friendship and support, and I thank God I've received them.

Revd John Newbury

✜ ✜ ✜

Facing reality, however painful and bumpy, is far healthier and holier than living with illusion.

Revd Murray Grant

✦ ✦ ✦

I really must pay tribute this morning to Donald Soper, who died yesterday at the age of ninety-five. A lifelong Methodist minister, supporter of radical causes and one of this century's greatest orators, he was certainly one of my heroes, particularly for his brilliant use of words.

He was perhaps best known for his open-air speaking in Hyde Park and on Tower Hill. He could draw a crowd, and keep them listening, better than any current politician, and he was perhaps the world's greatest expert at dealing with hecklers.

I'll give just one example: a man in the crowd once interrupted him by shouting, 'Christianity has been on the earth for two thousand years, and look at the state of the world today.'

'Sir,' replied Lord Soper. 'Water has been on the earth longer than that, and look at the colour of your neck.'

Captain Charles King

✢ ✢ ✢

I am proud to admit it, my grandparents were economic migrants. Actually, they were also fleeing from continual Jew-baiting as well as the grinding poverty of Eastern Europe, but it was the hope of a better life that brought them to these shores, and I hope all will agree, their descendants have added much to the vitality of this country.

So my blood boils when I hear the words 'asylum-seekers' and 'refugees' equated with 'cheats' and 'scroungers'. Most refugees don't just choose to up roots and go: they are driven here by different factors, both political and economic. And evidence seems to show that it is often the most ambitious who make it out. People who could add much to our society.

And I really don't understand the demand for proper papers. If you are expecting the dreaded midnight knock on the door, are you going to apply for legal government documents? It seems common sense to me that those who arrive without correct papers are most likely to be in need of asylum.

The story goes that one of my cousins was told on the Channel ferry that the polite answer to every question in English was 'cabbage'. Luckily the immigrant officer had compassion: told that the man's name was Cabbage, he issued papers in the name of Green. And Greens they have been ever since. But how Kosher could their papers have been for such a thing to happen?

The Bible teaches that you should love your neighbour as you love yourself. The absolute majority of those coming to this country are not bogus cheats, but good people seeking life and hope for themselves and their families. Like us …

The question is, can we still call ourselves a civilised community if we deny them dignity and support?

Rabbi Jackie Tabick

✢ ✢ ✢

Wherever there is pain in the body of humanity, even if it isn't in our neck of the woods, the resultant clenched fists affect us all. We see that in present world events. The purpose of prayer is to help us all stand upright, and not to remain uptight.

Revd Ruth Scott

✣ ✣ ✣

I thought of this the other day when I was doing one of my weekly family chores, the shopping. As I stood in the hypermarket, pondering the comparative merits of eight brands of ketchup, I was reminded of something my spiritual master taught me. He said we should see this world in the same way we see the goods in a shop. In a supermarket we know that everything belongs to someone else, that we must take only those things we need and can afford. In the same way, we should see that everything in this world belongs to God, and we should take only what we need. We can't just grab whatever we want. There is a price to pay.

The world's resources, if properly managed, can provide for everyone, probably ten times over. As Gandhi said, 'There is enough for everyone's need, but not for everyone's greed.'

Krishna Dharma

✛ ✛ ✛

I heard a story this week about a man who was walking through a busy city with a friend who had come up from the country. Suddenly the friend stopped and said, 'I can hear a grasshopper.'

'Don't be stupid,' said the man. 'We're in the middle of a city.' But his friend walked over to a huge plant standing in a pot outside a restaurant, and there in the leaves he found a grasshopper.

'How on earth did you hear that?' asked the man. 'No one else heard it.'

His friend took a coin out of his pocket and dropped it on to the pavement. Immediately, everyone within a hundred yards stopped and looked in the direction of the sound. We hear what we're tuned in to hearing.

People who pray get tuned in to God. And it's surprising how often we can hear him in our day-to-day lives.

Captain Charles King

✢ ✢ ✢

One thing you can say about John Wesley: he practised what he preached. Although he earned a lot of money himself by publishing books, he lived very simply and gave so much to the poor that he left only a few pounds and a couple of silver spoons behind him. So, there's some good advice for us all – gain all we can, save all we can, and give all we can.

Dr Pauline Webb

✤ ✤ ✤

It's said of Rabbi Roptchitz that he once came home from synagogue feeling rather stressed out. When his wife asked what the matter was he said, 'It's my sermon. I was talking about the importance of charity – how many poor and needy people there are and how the better off should give a little more.'

'And d'you think you were effective?' she asked.

'About half,' he answered. 'I think the have-nots are ready to receive – but I'm not sure whether the haves are ready to give!'

Angela Wood

✢ ✢ ✢

Don't judge the rich too harshly. When it comes to helping the poor, most of us are no better. Mother Teresa used to say, 'We should give until it hurts, otherwise it isn't charity, but justice.'

Fr Brian D'Arcy

✢ ✢ ✢

This is how morality evolves in Buddhism: you have to learn to think and reflect. To develop an awareness that everything we do has a consequence. Some have almost immediate effect, like the happiness of giving someone a gift. Some may take much longer, like the peace of a life well lived. And some we may never know.

Dharmachari Nagaraja

✣ ✣ ✣

My spiritual master, Srila Prabhupada, told a story of when he was a young man in India. In his village a girl became ill with typhoid. The doctor gave strict instructions that she should be given no food. But when her parents were out she begged her brother for something to eat. Feeling sorry for her, he gave her some bread, and her fever got worse. When the parents returned they were furious and they punished the boy. I will never forget Prabhupada's words: 'It was love,' he said, 'it was compassion, but the result was pain.'

Of course, the Hindu scriptures, the Vedas, instruct that we must look after the needy, but they say we should also know the ultimate reasons why need exists. I believe that this very knowledge is our real need, for once we have it we can end our suffering for ever.

Krishna Dharma

✢ ✢ ✢

According to the Torah, mankind wasn't made until the sixth day, but I believe that we're all partners with God in an ever-unfolding story of creation, and that there are always fresh opportunities for spiritual renewal. All too often people hear each other through a veil of their own fears and emotional scars, but we also have the capacity for repentance and reconciliation. There is only one way to end conflict: stop shouting at the past! Let go of pointless grudges and poisonous hatreds. It's never too late to heal rifts and start again. If necessary, over and over until the end of time.

Naomi Gryn

✢ ✢ ✢

I love the African story of the farmer who brought home a little chick from an eagle's nest. He put it in a chicken run where it grew up with the chickens. One day a passing traveller called by and commented on its presence.

'It's a chicken,' said the farmer.

'Not so,' said the traveller, 'it's an eagle.' He took hold of the bird and, placing it on his wrist, he commanded it to fly. Nothing happened.

The farmer was delighted. 'See, I told you so, it's a chicken.'

The traveller returned daily to feed the little bird with food fit for an eagle. Each time he tried to get the bird to fly, but seeing the chickens scratching in the run it would hop down and scratch with them. One morning, very early, the traveller took the little bird away from the rest of the brood and told it, 'You are an eagle, fly; you are an eagle, fly.' With that, the great bird looked up, stretched its wings and flew.

How I wish that we all had someone in our lives who would encourage us to 'fly' and not just settle for second best or for the crumbs which fall from others' tables. Quite the opposite is true, however. I see so many people who are content to settle for crumbs. Not only do they surround themselves with negative beliefs, but they also have a low expectation about life and what is possible for them. Their password is 'I can't'.

A wind of change is needed in order to create or recreate a belief in ourselves which begins to say, 'Yes, I can'; space must be made for this belief to well up inside us, until it becomes a reality.

Revd Rose Hudson-Wilkin

✢ ✢ ✢

This week in synagogue we will be reading how God rescued the Jews from slavery in Egypt, carrying us off on eagles' wings. The rabbis asked, 'Why eagles? How come they had the pleasure?'

Now I doubt the accuracy of their ornithological knowledge, but the reason one of the sages gives for the choice is wonderful.

He asked, 'How are eagles different from all other birds?' All other birds carry their young between their feet, because they are afraid of the birds who fly above them. But the eagle is only afraid of men who might shoot at him, and therefore he carries his young on his wings because he prefers to have the arrows lodge in him rather than in his children.

Rabbi Jackie Tabick

✥ ✥ ✥

A visitor to Africa noted how an African woman farmer bowed respectfully to the land and asked permission to take food from it. That's a sharp reminder that the earth – which is the Lord's – is a gift to us and we mustn't squander it.

Revd John Newbury

❖ ❖ ❖

There is, apparently, a coastline where, from time to time, great quantities of starfish become beached. Hundreds and hundreds of them, completely stranded.

One day a man was walking along the beach when he discovered a young boy busily picking up the starfish, one at a time, running with them down to the water's edge, and pushing them safely back into the sea.

The man watched for a while and then

asked the boy, 'Why are you doing that? There are thousands of them. What you're doing won't make any difference, you know.'

The lad didn't answer immediately. He simply picked up another starfish, ran to the sea and put it back in.

'It will to that one,' he said.

Captain Charles King

❖ ❖ ❖

A Himalayan parable: a man was walking in the mountains, and in the distance he saw a fearsome beast rushing towards him. Naturally he turned and ran for his life. After a while, he glanced over his shoulder and was horrified to see the creature gaining on him. Then, as he looked back again, he was relieved to see that it wasn't a beast but a man. He continued to run, and then, exhausted, stopped and turned. The man had almost caught up with him. But then to his joy he saw it wasn't any man. It was his own brother.

Indarjit Singh

✥ ✥ ✥

Impermanence is all around us. It is there in the passing clouds and the fall of summer rain. The truth of it cannot harm you, but free you to live each day with wonder and gratitude.

Dharmachari Nagaraja

✥ ✥ ✥

One of the most endearing characteristics of Queen Elizabeth, the Queen Mother was her sense of fun and her capacity to make everybody feel totally at ease in her company.

Less than a year ago I had the privilege of being next to her at a luncheon party. We talked about all sorts of things and began reminiscing about the Second World War. We found ourselves humming the old popular tunes like 'The White Cliffs of Dover' and 'We'll Meet Again (Don't know where, don't know when)'. Soon the whole table was joining in and it became a luncheon singsong.

Suddenly the Queen Mother started to sing a song called 'Taxi', and she sang it very well. When she finished I said to her, 'Ma'm, I must confess that I have never heard that song before,' and she smiled and said, 'No you wouldn't have – it was a hit tune in 1910!'

I suppose it is a gift given to old people

that they remember things not just in the immediate past, but even more vividly in the distant past. So it was with Queen Elizabeth, the Queen Mother. She had a memory of events which stretched back to the early years of the twentieth century: things both good and bad; war and peace; extraordinary scientific progress; and also the deep things that bind us all – passion, pain, sorrow, joy, achievement, friendship, love.

Today we remember the Queen Mother and give thanks for the pleasure, the tradition and the devoted service she gave to all in this country and beyond.

We all have our own personal memories of good times and bad and sometimes we are tempted to feel a touch nostalgic – and why not? But we should also remember to look forward and to do so in a spirit of hope, because this is not only our world, with our memories; it is also God's world. He has a purpose for each and everyone of us. And it matters how each of us chooses to live our life. Or rather, it matters that we strive to live as God wants us to live.

Today we pray for the Queen Mother. We give thanks to God that she was not just a great and gracious lady but one of us. And we pray that the Lord will say to her, in the words of the Gospel, 'Well done thou good and faithful servant … enter into the joy of the Lord.'

Cardinal Cormac Murphy O'Connor

✤ ✤ ✤

BIOGRAPHICAL NOTES

Faris Badawi is the administrator of the Muslim
College in London.

Rt Revd George Carey is the Archbishop of
Canterbury.

Father Brian D'Arcy is a Passionist priest from
Ireland.

Krishna Dharma is a Vaishnava priest, author and
consultant on Hinduism.

Revd Joel Edwards is the General Director of the
Evangelical Alliance.

Revd Robert Gillion is an Anglican vicar in
Chelsea and Advisor to the Bishop of
Kensington on Evangelism.

Revd Murray Grant is an Anglican priest. He is
Chaplain to the British Forces at NATO in
Naples.

Naomi Gryn is a writer and film-maker.

Revd Rose Hudson-Wilkin is an Anglican priest

and Vicar of Holy Trinity Dalston and All Saints Hagerston.

Revd Paul Hulme is a Methodist minister based in London.

Yusuf Islam is a writer and educationalist living in London.

Revd Roy Jenkins is a Baptist minister living in Wales.

Captain Charles King is the editor of the Salvation Army's *The Salvationist*.

Oliver McTernan is a a Fellow at the Harvard Centre for International Affairs in Boston.

Fidelma Meehan is Projects Co-ordinator for the Bahái community in Swindon.

Cardinal Cormac Murphy O'Connor is the Roman Catholic Archbishop of Westminster.

Dharmachari Nagaraja is a member of the London Buddhist Centre.

Revd John Newbury is a Methodist minister who has worked at the World Council of Churches in Geneva.

Revd John Rackley is Minister at Manvers Street Baptist Church, Bath.

Canon Roger Royle is an Anglican priest. He is Presenter of BBC Radio 2's *Sunday Half Hour*.

Revd Ruth Scott is an Anglican priest in Richmond.

Indarjit Singh is editor of *The Sikh Messenger* and a member of the Sikh Council for Inter Faith Relations.

Rabbi Jackie Tabick is Rabbi of the North-West Surrey Synagogue, Vice President of the Reform Synagogues of Great Britain and Chair of the World Congress of Faiths.

Dr Pauline Webb is a Methodist lay preacher and former Head of Religion for BBC World Service.

Rt Revd Roy Williamson is the former Anglican Bishop of Southwark.

Angela Wood is an Orthodox Jew living in London.